Just the Opposite

Up
Down

Sharon Gordon

BENCHMARK BOOKS

MARSHALL CAVENDISH
NEW YORK

The kite is up.

The kite is down.

The dog is up.

The dog is down.

The ball is up.

The ball is down.

The cat is up.

The cat is down.

The girl is up.

The girl is down.

The frog is up.

The frog is down.

The balloon is up.

The balloon is down.

The seesaw is up.

The seesaw is down.

The boy is up.

Come down!

Words We Know

ball

balloon

boy

cat

dog

frog

girl

kite

seesaw

Index

Page numbers in **boldface** are illustrations.

About the Author

Sharon Gordon has written many books for young children. She has also worked as an editor. Sharon and her husband Bruce have three children, Douglas, Katie, and Laura, and one spoiled pooch, Samantha. They live in Midland Park, New Jersey.

With thanks to Nanci Vargus, Ed.D.
and Beth Walker Gambro, reading consultants

Benchmark Books
Marshall Cavendish
99 White Plains Road
Tarrytown, New York 10591-9001
www.marshallcavendish.com

Library of Congress Cataloging-in-Publication Data

Gordon, Sharon.
Up down / by Sharon Gordon.
p. cm. — (Bookworms: Just the opposite)
Includes index.
Summary: Provides examples of people, animals,
and objects in motion to demonstrate the concept of up and down.
ISBN 0-7614-1573-4
1. English language—Synonyms and antonyms—Juvenile literature. [1.
English language—Synonyms and antonyms. 2. Animals.] I. Title II.
Series: Gordon, Sharon. Bookworms: Just the opposite.

PE1591.G638 2003
428.1—dc21
2003010079

Photo Research by Anne Burns Images

Cover Photos: *Corbis*: (up-Royalty Free), (down-Tim Davis)
The photographs in this book are used with permission and through the courtesy *cri, Inc.*: pp. 1 (left), 4 Wachter; pp. 1 (right), 5, 20 (bottom right) Bonnie Sue Ranch; pp. 2, 3, 21 (top right, *otopic*; p. 6 James Kirby; pp. 7, 20 (top left) Brian Drake. *Corbis*: pp. 8, 10, 21 (bottom left) Royalty Free; pp. 9, 20 (bottom middle) Tim Davis; p. 11 Cat Gwynn; pp. 14, 20 (bottom left) Paul A. Souders; p. 15 Bosco Laura/Sygma; pp. 18, 20 (top right) Laura Doss. *Animals Animals*: pp. 12, 13, 21 (top left) Stephen Dalton. *Photo Edit*: pp. 16, 17, 21 (bottom right) Myrleen Ferguson Cate. *SWA Photo*: p. 19.

Series design by Becky Terhune

Printed in China
1 3 5 6 4 2